PHILIP PEARLSTEIN

PHILIP PEARLSTEIN

THE YELLOW GLASSES

Jim Dicke II

Orange *frazer* Press
Wilmington, Ohio

For Janet

INTRODUCTION

When Philip Pearlstein agreed to paint a portrait of Jim Dicke, he gained not only a patient sitter but also an insightful artistic biographer. Dicke's account of his experience sitting for Pearlstein offers many new details of the artist's working method, while also opening the door to understanding every artist's essential concerns. Pearlstein was meticulous in establishing Dicke's commitment to each aspect of the project, and Dicke in turn carefully details the myriad ways the artist's intentionality was revealed. Dicke conveys the workaday aspects of the artist's practice even as he illuminates the much larger enterprise of capturing a likeness that is partly a personal response to the sitter and partly an expression of the artist's inner world.

Dicke's inspired understanding of Pearlstein's art was only possible because he, too, is a painter with near-daily studio work over several decades. He occasionally offers background on historical practices, which helps situate Pearlstein among the larger cohort of realist painters who work in that liminal space between objective representation and the abstract space of two dimensions. Because Dicke is himself completely at home with a paintbrush, these ideas flow naturally through the narrative.

Dicke never divulges to the reader his own painting experience, presenting himself merely as a supportive collector. His essay is wholly in the service of Pearlstein and his art, inspired by his enormous regard for the artist. He vowed to be Pearlstein's "most cooperative unpaid model ever," a long process allowing for the relationship to "evolve into a celebration of a new friendship and a deepening of my admiration for this good man."

Ultimately, Dicke's account tells how *two* good men discovered each other. The unfolding story rewards the reader in so many ways, artistic and personal. Dicke reminds all of us that artists are deeply engaged in a mysterious world, and he gives us a fascinating glimpse through the portal.

—Elizabeth Broun
Director Emerita
Smithsonian American Art Museum

Knowing of my admiration for Philip Pearlstein and knowing of Philip's pleasure at doing the occasional portrait, my friend Jaime Frankfurt mentioned to me, and to Philip Pearlstein's dealer, Betty Cuningham, mentioned to Philip, that perhaps Philip might paint my portrait. From there, the suggestion took on a life of its own. I'm not sure there was even a moment of conscience decision. What I do know is that the portrait was not commissioned for a particular place, purpose, or to commemorate any rite of passage one normally associates with the commissioning of a portrait. If anything, it evolved into a celebration of a new friendship and a deepening of my admiration for this good man.

Initially, I remember Jaime saying he thought a first step before I should decide, or before Philip should commit, would be for us to meet one another. Would I like to go to Philip's studio on 33rd Street? Of course! I would be honored to meet him. Philip was one of the great artists of our age. It would be a pleasure.

An afternoon appointment was set. Philip painted in the natural morning light and did his best to reserve mornings for painting time. As one reads about the lives of painters, one of the reoccurring themes is the distractions that come to pull the artist away from studio time. Artists who are struggling financially have other jobs to keep food on the table and find their schedule is likely not their own. Also, the extraordinarily successful artist is pressed to promote his work, meet with collectors, sit on boards and speak, teach, or make appearances. It all conspires to deprive the artist of precious time to focus on making art. Picasso even famously adopted a working method where he painted at night under harsh, flat, artificial light and only had certain hours in the afternoon when he would be available to meet visitors. An artist needs to guard the studio schedule carefully or time gets pre-empted.

From the first meeting, I liked Philip and his wife Dorothy very much and I assumed the meeting was mostly about seeing if there was personal chemistry. Some artists have a hard time painting someone they don't find interesting or at least sympathetic. Some subjects have a problem sitting for an artist who wants to work directly from the presence of the sitter. Even a prop can look different in the absence of the sitter and these are things most sitters might not realize. When this happens, the mutual discomfort, if it develops, can show on the finished canvas. I now think I was wrong and in that first meeting, Philip was more concerned with the amount of sitting time I would be willing to commit and wanted something of a face-to-face conversation on the matter. He stressed in our interview that three or four sessions of two hours each should be enough, but it might slip into a fifth session. When I assured him this would not be a problem, he still seemed uncertain. I am sure it was a hesitancy born of past experience.

The tour of his studio was like something I had not seen with any other artist. The Pearlsteins had an apartment with a living room and kitchen that was at once modest and exquisite. Like many well-educated people who are passionate about the arts, their taste level was clearly thoughtful about every item. The studio itself sprawled across the entire floor of the building. The part not devoted to the Pearlsteins apartment was devoted to Philip's art. There were several tableaus assembled with work in progress, carefully orchestrated Pearlsteins curated minus only the models. Small pieces of tape on the wooden floor were there to place an item perfectly again if it got bumped out of its place. When I was there, one was a most unique Pearlstein painting in an early stage of progress. It contained a neon light Mickey Mouse with a blow-up clear swimming pool chair.[1] The effect was truly unique.

Pearlstein had a woman, Jamie MacKenzie, working at the studio in a freestanding office cubicle documenting the *catalogue raisonné* of his life's work and writings while facilitating his current correspondence. At least this was my impression of her work day. She would answer the phone, take messages, and help channel Philip's work day to minimize interruption and distraction. I got the impression she was playing catch-up from years of Philip's work not having the luxury of careful cataloging.

Another revelation was the extent to which Philip had collected and retained most of the objects and props he had used in his artworks over the years. There was a plethora of toys and carpets, chairs, antiques, and little treasures.[2] A personal passion was the collection of ancient pottery, shards, and figures. I understand the fascination though I don't have it myself. To hold a little ceramic oil lamp in your hand that was lighting some space at night two-thousand years ago holds a kind of magic. While the world has continued to advance technologically at an ever-quickening pace, there is still a strong connection to our fascination with these objects from another age.

Pearlstein said he had been considering doing my portrait as a three-quarter length image on a vertical canvas, about 48 x 36, and what did I think? I told him that sounded good and there we had it. I had never really come to the conclusion that our family, anyone for that matter, had a particular need for my portrait. I am not aware that his dealer was in the habit of seeking portrait commissions. Yet there we were. All that was left to do was to set a time for our first sitting.

Philip asked how I wanted to be dressed and I suggested the same kind of informal garb Jaime Frankfurt and I normally wore as we tramped the corridors of museums and galleries. I usually wore black jeans with a dress shirt and sport coat, or sweater if it was chilly. Philip suggested a necktie and I offered to bring several, so he could make a choice. I offered to bring one of our chairs from home but he dismissed the possibility, saying if I did not mind, he wanted to use one of his own chairs from his own collection. He had several things on the calendar—an upcoming show—and he needed time to have a canvas made. He was just finishing one of his projects, a work that would eventually go to the Smithsonian American Art Museum. He would let me know when we could schedule an initial sitting.

A few weeks later, Philip's office called mine in Ohio and we made our first appointment. I was going to be in New York City that week anyway, but Philip seemed surprised that the first time he had suggested for a sitting would work just fine for me.

I arrived at the appointed hour of 10:00 am and as I came in the ground level door, two young women in blue jeans and zipper jackets with big purses came giggling down the stairs looking like a couple of art students. It only occurred to me later that they were probably two of Philip's models departing from their sitting session. By my count in the coming months, I would sit for Philip thirty-nine and one-half hours, developing the kind of regard and affection for him that one has for a godfather or a favorite uncle. I never crossed paths with a model again after that first day.

I put some thought into what I would wear and I decided on black Levi-brand jeans. One of my favorite kinds of shirt is a Brooks Brothers light blue permanent-press shirt, with a button-down collar. For five years at Culver Military Academy, I had worn a blue chambray shirt as a part of the uniform each day and had grown to like them. The color wears well and doesn't look dingy as it gets older. Philip liked the idea that I would not wear a sport coat, or a sweater, or a "blue scarf," but was keen on the idea of a necktie as a compositional element to "divide the canvas" in two hemispheres as he put it. As promised, I brought several neckties to give him a selection. As I put on the one he liked best, I asked if he wanted it tied but loose, with an open collar, or did he want the knot pulled up in its proper place. "Oh," he said, "let's do it with an open collar."

The chair he had chosen was a black Windsor chair he had placed in an area near a north-facing window but with an artificial light source set up, as well. The chair was on a riser only a couple of inches tall. He had his paints on a cart with a pallet that seemed to be an enamel steel tray. I learned later the tray had come years earlier from the famous "Automat" restaurant. It seemed a bit low to me for it to be a comfortable working height but then it struck me for the first time how short Philip was. I knew that I was taller than Philip, the way we all have some vague idea we are taller than, or shorter than, or the same size as someone we know, but sitting on that chair with us eye-to-eye was the first time I truly realized his height.

The canvas was a beautifully made white linen canvas without a colored surface. Some artists like a colored primer in light gray or brown, and I had even heard one artist say a tinted canvas is like playing the piano from the center of the keyboard, instead of trying to play it with the stool up at E over High C.

He started with a delicate piece of charcoal and sketched freehand on the canvas itself, and spent that first session getting me and the chair down on that canvas in rough outline, using only his eyes and the charcoal. There would be no photograph, no projection, and no plumb bob, but only his eyes, his right hand, and his arm, with occasional long, broad sweeps, sketching right on the canvas, while we struck up a conversation and started to get to know one another.

My shoes were not going to show in the portrait but I wore the same pair of black loafers each time. In addition to my wedding ring, I wore the watch my wife, Janet, had given me for my 60th birthday, a watch with special sentiment, since she had made a point of finding an old Rolex model called a Bubbleback made in the year of my birth, 1945. The final piece of significance I chose was a Texas belt buckle with my initials "JFD," which had been a 21st birthday present. A lifelong Ohio resident, I'd been born in Texas, gone to Culver in Indiana, then back to Texas for college at Trinity University. For a portrait without a lot of props, I thought at least some personal touches had been given a passing nod. The yellow glasses were an honor that would come later.[3]

I had read a little about Pearlstein's life and career and, of course, people were always talking about the Warhol connection. Philip and Andy went to art school in Philadelphia and both decided to come to New York to try their hand at making a living in the art business. Philip was a veteran of World War II and already married, and while he and Warhol literally got on the train together to ride from Philadelphia to New York, and had gone to art school together, their career efforts took very different paths.[4] From the beginning, Pearlstein initially focused less on advertising work. While they maintained their friendship, neither ever became a footnote for the other.

I returned for my second sitting a week later and was most curious to see what had happened since my last visit. Little pieces of tape now marked the placement of the platform on the floor and the chair on the platform. He had me resume my arrangement in the chair and then spent a little time adjusting the light and adjusting the placement of his paints, brushes, and table. There was a tense moment where you could see all the thinking about his intentionality coming into play. At a baseball game, you can watch a great pitcher have that moment of reflection just before he pitches the ball where he thinks about where he wants it to go and in what way and at what speed before muscle memory kicks in. It was that sort of intention that settled on his face at the first part of this second session.

He had clearly not touched the canvas since I was last there in what I soon observed was his pattern between all our sessions. When one is putting one color of paint against another and trying to capture shadows and highlights, the color you put down now affects how you see the color you put down next to it just a short time ago, and back and forth.

He mixed a flesh tone and he mixed a whitish black. He looked intently at the canvas, put down the brush, picked up a cloth and wiped away the charcoal sketch he had done a week earlier, leaving only the faintest outline to help himself along. Then he started painting on the face and hair, laying down a likeness that he would develop with more subtlety in subsequent sessions but not really change.

Some artists don't want you to see work in progress, and certainly don't want to explain or defend what they are doing as a painting is in progress, but Philip was not that way. He was happy for me to see what he had done at the end of each session and seemed pleased that I offered only words of approval. In truth, at the end of that painting session, I was pleased with the kind, grey-white color he'd chosen for my hair and saw that the light placement had put some shadows across my brow that weren't really there to my way of thinking. We never see ourselves as other more objective observers see us.

On an earlier tour, one of the paintings he had been working on was of two ladies reclining in a still life. They were not engaged with the viewer or even engaged with each other, but central to the composition was a large contemporary wristwatch on one woman's wrist.[5] The painting was complete now and on an easel behind Philip facing me, either serving as a light reflector for him or as something to draw my attention, so I would keep my head still. I was not sure which. I looked at the models in the painting and wondered if they were the two young art students I'd seen leaving the studio that first day.

The next two-hour session took a surprise turn. Philip painted the left side only of my shirt (on the right side of the canvas). Not a speck of paint did he put on the other side of the shirt or lay down a tone for anything else. It was as if he did not care to put down painting he would later refine, but only wanted to paint a mostly finished single piece of a painting in one go each time as if pieces of a jigsaw puzzle were being assembled one piece at a time.

The next session happened on a grey day and I thought my shirt looked a little different in the grey light. As he painted, Philip started talking about his experience painting Henry Kissinger. He talked about Dr. Kissinger being a pleasant man with a good sense of humor and how instead of Dr. Kissinger coming to the studio, Philip had been asked to go to Dr. Kissinger's office. There had not been room in the office for Philip to get very far back when as he was painting. Dr. Kissinger had been sitting at the desk most of the time, going through papers and taking phone calls, so it had been difficult to have him hold still long enough to paint light and shadow. "How long did he give you?" I asked, to which Philip said, "I think only about three hours." Later, I would see the portrait of Dr. Kissinger by Pearlstein at the Smithsonian American Art Museum and I could see the issue. While the work has a wonderful spontaneous quality, the big square canvas is a close up of Dr. Kissinger's animated head and shoulders, a wonderful work of art, but more lacking in detail than a fully-resolved Pearlstein work.

As he finished the story on Dr. Kissinger, it dawned on me, perhaps, why I was being told the story. This was Session Three, and he had originally said three or four sessions or five sessions were all he would need.

Slowly, my realization had come together. His normal way of working was to hire models by the hour and have them sit for as many sessions as it took for him to be satisfied with the finished work. When he was doing a portrait, he might feel pressures from the sitter to work in a way that he knew was not optimal for him. I silently resolved, right then, to try to be his most cooperative unpaid model ever.

Our talks were wide ranging. Knowing that I was a business person, an art collector, and involved in the museum world, gave us hours of conversation about the dilemmas he faced with the inventory of his own art and props when he and Dorothy would be gone. His son is an attorney and was helping him. He spoke fondly of his family. I remember thinking the artistic legacy of artistic parents can be both a blessing and a challenge for families. I sympathized with his concern for the challenge to come.

Philip talked about his art history thesis and while I don't remember all he said about it, he clearly talked of it in terms of a set of ideas that became central to his own art choices throughout his career.[6] I said I would enjoy reading it if I could borrow a copy and that I would return it the next week. He said he was not sure where it was but he would look, and at our next session he loaned me what he said was his last copy. I treated it with great care and even had a few duplicates made for him.

For a time, the painting seemed to go much more quickly and I thought it would come to a close sooner than it actually ended up needing. In one session he did the background and most of the chair, not touching the figure. In another session he did my hands, and then in another used a session to paint the necktie.

In the meantime, I discovered Brooks Brothers does indeed have two shirts, which are ever so slightly different shades of blue—one called Oxford Light Blue and one called Oxford

Blue. It seemed that on the successive days when the two sides of my shirt were being painted, I had inadvertently worn the two different shades of blue. As the painting progressed, this got resolved, but initially you could clearly see the two sides of the shirt were different. A little embarrassed, I never confessed my mistake to Philip and he never asked.

I started saving the necktie for sittings so that it would not get soiled and showed up for one of the sittings wearing a different tie, which I started to remove in order to put on the correct tie for the painting. Philip stopped me, saying he liked this new tie better and would I mind if he used it for the portrait, as well. Of course I agreed, and that day we spent the entire sitting with him painting over the "old" necktie with the "new" one. At the end of the sitting I realized he had been totally correct in a very subtle way. It is impossible for me to articulate how, but the change of necktie had made a meaningful difference to the painting.

The friendship deepened. Philip invited me to attend the National Academy of Arts and Letters as his guest and I enjoyed a lovely evening in their apartment where Dorothy offered me a glass of wine and I admired one of Philip's paintings hanging over the couch. Dorothy said, "It is one of my favorites, too. You should talk to Betty Cuningham. We would sell it." And so I spoke with Betty, with several works eventually coming into our collection, including the one over the couch, and I also made gifts of his work to the National Gallery and to the Smithsonian American Art Museum.[7]

Philip was an artist who had been generous with his own time over the years as a supporter of the larger art world. He had served as a commissioner at the Smithsonian and also as the president of the National Academy of Arts and Letters. He spoke with me of the task he had undertaken to review and rationalize some of the Arts and Letters artistic bequests. Such a thing is no small effort. He shared stories of the pleasure he and Dorothy enjoyed at their lake home and how much enjoyment he got from the quiet exercise of paddling a kayak.

At one sitting, I arrived to find a huge hole in the 33rd Street pavement which had been created by a broken city service main. Philip was unphased by the street next to his building having collapsed into a deep hole.

On only one occasion did either of us cancel a sitting. My office got a call from Philip's assistant, saying he would need to reschedule since he had been rushed to the hospital with a heart issue. The next week, however, he rescheduled and was back at work telling me about the installation of a heart stent, as if it was just another trip to the dentist or something. He was incredibly persistent and focused.

At the end of the process, he said, "If you can stay a bit longer today, I think we can finish."[8] He had decided he wanted to paint my reading glasses hanging from my pocket and he chose to use this final session to do what he called "my Vermeer thing." About three hours later, he said, "Well, I think it's done." He called Dorothy to offer her critique. I told him I thought it was wonderful. In truth, I did think he had created a great painting, but truly I liked the man so much I would have made supportive noises no matter what, rather than hurt his feelings.

Philip and I remained friends. Occasionally, I would send wine, we would talk on the phone, or I would come to one of his openings.[9] He had done a little watercolor self portrait in 2012 which I felt lucky to acquire at one of his last shows. And while being ninety-eight and vigorous to the end must count as an amazing victory, I miss him and the keen loss was like losing a favorite friend.[10]

I will never forget standing with him looking at the painting he was doing of the inflatable chair and the neon Mickey Mouse when the models were not there but the props were all in place and the canvas half finished. He looked up at my six-foot self and said, "You know, some critics think my figures are out of proportion, but because of my height, that is how I see them. Put your head down at my level and look." I did, and Philip was so correct. From his vantage point, one could look around the room and the whole world looked like a Pearlstein. The man was great. It was magical. I miss my friend.

1 *Two Models with Balloon Chair and Mickey Mouse* in progress in the studio as the Dicke portrait was also underway.

2 *Model with Japanese Lantern and Folk Art Horse* from one of his last shows.

3 *Jim Dicke II*

4   *The Ridge,* 1955. Philip told me this series of his early work was actually based on scholars rocks.

[5] *The Flying Goose Decoy* just completed as he was about to begin the Dicke portrait. Philip had tried to purchase the model's watch from her for his collection of props.

6 *View Toward Positano, The Siren Islands.* Painted at the site, 1973.

7   *Two Models with Sudanese Antelope, Carrousel Lion and Ikat Rug* first seen over Philip and Dorothy's couch.

22   JIM DICKE II

[8] *Untitled (Nude and Butterfly)* a gift from Philip at our last sitting.

⁹ *Cast Iron Owl Andirons,* 2020. By coincidence, we have a pair of owl fireplace andirons like these which made it poignant as one of our final purchases from one of his final shows.

[10] *Self Portrait,* 2012 purchased from Betty Cunningham.

ISBN 978-1949248-838
Copyright ©2024 Crown Equipment Corporation
All Rights Reserved

No part of this publication may be reproduced in any material form (including photocopying or storing in any medium by electronic means and whether or not transiently or incidentally to some other use of this publication) without the written permission of the copyright holder except in accordance with the provisions of Title 17 of the United States Code.

Published for the copyright holder by:
Orange Frazer Press
37½ West Main St.
P.O. Box 214
Wilmington, OH 45177

For price and shipping information, call: 937.382.3196
Or visit: www.orangefrazer.com

Book and cover design:
Orange Frazer Press with Catie South

Library of Congress Control Number: 2024901398

First Printing